SOMETHING AB

BRIST

Memories of life in the city
from the 1920's to today

REDCLIFFE

Bristol

First published in 1989 by
Redcliffe Press Ltd, 49 Park Street, Bristol 1

ISBN 0 948265 09 4

*Printed in Great Britain by
WBC Print Ltd, Bristol*

Contents

Cuckoo Lane

Fred Catley

I was born in a house which no longer exists, in country which has long since disappeared—on June 14th, 1911, a hot summer, at 1 Cuckoo Lane, St George, near the Kingswood boundary. Kingswood was in Gloucestershire, we were just inside the City and County of Bristol. It was the corner house at the end of a terrace of Victorian cottages, where Cuckoo Lane joined Black Boy and Trumpet Lane, part of which, with a covered well, was sometimes called Old Pump Lane. The lanes were narrow and rough, with hedges and elm trees. Swan Lane had a pond part way down, with trees round it and a house. Past this, the lane widened, with others joining it, and became Hillside Road, still there, with Air Balloon School. A redbrick wall inside Swan Lane hedge showed that widening had been planned but was abandoned during World War I. I remember stone stiles and fields and footpaths. New roads and houses between the Wars destroyed all the home-country of my childhood.

My father was a clerk at G.B. Britton's boot-factory in Kingswood. I can hardly remember him. He was killed in World War I, in August 1917, 'near Arras', said a memorial stone, to him and to his parents, in Radstock churchyard. I must have been only five when I last saw him, before he went off to his death in that appalling War, which in some families wiped out all their sons and made innumerable orphans. We were three, brother Will and sister Gladys before me. Our mother was always grateful to Britton's for paying her a weekly pension of 12/6 (62½p) till she died, only 56, in 1931. My father married her on a wage of £1 a week. When he left for the War, his wage was thirty shillings (£1.50). So, as a war-widow with pension and small allowances for three children and 12/6 from Britton's, she was at least no worse off after the War, but the loss to us all was more than I can ever know. My father was an intelligent man. He left some writings—*A Statement of Faith* and *My Utopia*—about the better life he had hoped for. Like others of his generation, he believed 'These things shall be! A loftier race than e're the world hath known shall rise', in the words of John Addington Symonds. Material conditions and medical care have improved immeasurably, yet the 'loftier race' and the lovelier kinder world they dreamed of are still far away. Evil has changed its face, that's all.

It must be impossible for most people today to understand how we lived then, without constant hot water, radio, television and with very few cars. Our water came from an outside tap with an old brown sink, and rain-water well with bucket to draw water for a zinc bath used in front of the living-room fire. That fire, burning in summer as in winter, with black hobs and oven and fire-guard, was the only source of heat, kettles and saucepans

4

providing hot water. Yet we considered ourselves 'comfortable'. I remember seeing ragged barefoot children in Castle Street, Bristol's busiest shopping street (World War II bombs wiped it out). Our rare visits to 'town' were by electric tram, for though we were surrounded by fields the main road from Bristol to Kingswood, with tramlines all the way, was near. Later, as a day-boy at Queen Elizabeth's Hospital on Brandon Hill, I became too familiar with cold, wet, windy journeys on the open tops of those trams, which we called 'cars'. Seats on top were made so that when wet they could be turned over to the dry side and reversed themselves when you got up—ingenious, but small compensation for sitting in cold wind and rain through a long journey. The driver was worse off. He stood without shelter, just changing ends for each journey—front and back were the same in a tram. The inside had a long seat on each side, with an aisle down the middle, crammed with standing passengers in wet weather.

I knew a tram-driver, Mr Kelly, who later succeeded in changing to a double-decker 'bus. He had ten children. Two young sons, 'the Kelly brothers', played violins at meetings. Sometimes I played piano with them. Music was self-made then, often centred round local chapels. My grandfather, born at Writhlington in 1830, was a Methodist local preacher. My father, though more socialist than Methodist, had played harmonium in chapels. He left at his death a harmonium and music—oratorios, song-books and *The Harmonium Cabinet*, a book of well-known Victorian tunes. I wish I had it still. When, aged 18, I at last acquired a piano, the old Harmonium was sold. The book went with it.

Music has been perhaps my greatest pleasure. I learned to read music, in six months of weekly lessons, sixpence each, from an elderly tobacconist, 'Professor' Lloyd. Sometimes his wife took the lessons, as she and their adult son played piano and violin too. That is all the musical tuition I ever had—books did the rest—but it gave me a lifetime of music-making.

Near their shop was the barber's, old Mr Harding's, enlivened by caged birds; canaries, goldfinches, linnets, birds it would now be illegal to cage. A notice said: GENTLEMEN DO NOT SPIT. OTHERS MUST NOT.

My elementary school, Two Mile Hill, was close to the smithy in grim Skulls Barton. I remember the glowing furnace, red-hot horse-shoes, patient horses and the two aproned smiths. From there, Reformatory Road led down to the high-walled school for delinquent boys.

The great change came when a new road was driven through between school and church, swallowing Blackboy and Trumpet Lane, to the Hanham main road. It was called Kingsway. Our house came down, but we had moved next door, when the Brooms migrated to Canada. For a time we still had country around us. The life of the fields and trees—little owls, swallows, cuckoos, warblers, haymaking—ebbed away as new houses were built.

Leaving school in 1928, I went to George's, the Park Street booksellers, and was interviewed by old Charles George, the surviving son of 'William George's Sons Ltd.' He looked at my address. 'Cuckoo Lane—I see that people there are asking to have the name changed. I think it's a pretty name.' So did I, but alas! the newcomers succeeded in having it altered to 'Kingsway Avenue.' Goodbye, Cuckoo Lane! I'm glad I was born there.

Those were the days

Danny Price

I was born in a district of Bristol with the saintly name of St Philips. Like many other parts of Bristol at that time, it bore a saintly name for deathly surroundings; St Judes, St Pauls, St James and Temple. All slums with hellish dwellings.

It was a valley, south of Old Market Street comprising a manure works, several knackers' yards, a gas works, coal wharves, soap works, a cattle market, tatters yards, brewery, burial ground, railway junctions, iron and steel works and also two good businesses producing custard powder and pork pies and sausages. Through the middle flowed the Cut, the River Avon, a tidal river into which was directed the human excrement of the population which, when the tide was out, rested on muddy banks. The tide would flow inland and out again towards the sea like a huge lavatory flush depositing its contents through South Bristol and the picturesque Avon Gorge to the sea adjacent to the well known health resorts of Weston-super-Mare and Clevedon. Alongside this was the Feeder Canal and into its placid waters was spewed the waste of the industries previously mentioned.

The environment was the natural selection for a number of inhabitants such as 50,000 rats, 100,000 bugs and in the summer was an idyllic abode for millions of flies. The habitat also included 15,000 human beings; men, women and children being born, educated, working, marrying, reproducing and dying in these surroundings. The houses were mostly two up and two down. Situated in narrow streets, occupying the minimum of space, alleyways or courtyards, it would seem as though the builders of the hovels originally endeavoured as far as possible to shut out the light and sun to the unfortunate tenants. None of the houses had inside toilets or bathrooms, the majority had no running water, no electric or gas light, cooking was performed over an open fire and oven. The tenants' needs for elimination were catered for by an outside box-like structure—just sufficient space for only the normal sized person to squat in comfort. It was pretty awkward for the fatties, especially for the overweight ladies with extensive outsize dresses and those long drawers. Washing, for the ladies, involved the use of a bucket or bowl filled from the tap outside. The males usually washed underneath the tap. This outside water tap, as well as the outside toilets, would have to serve the physical needs of several houses in a small street, alley or courtyard. I cannot remember any house in St Philips that had a bathroom and the bathing of the family was carried out—a Saturday night ritual—in a large tin bath, with the water being heated over the open fire in large kettles. When not in use, the tin bath was hung on a large nail hammered to the lavatory. The washing of one's clothes was a one day weekly chore. The wash house, containing a large copper with an open fire and a wooden bench was used by several families—each house having its own particular day.

The wash day started with the lighting of the fire with sticks and coal to heat the water into which all the dirty clothes were put and boiled together with liberal sprinklings of soda. The clothes were then taken out of the

copper and scrubbed with a hard hand brush over a board on the wooden bench with Sunlight soap.

With a large family this took all day and it was a hard, uncomfortable task. I can still see my mother's hands after a day's wash—red, chapped and bleeding with the effects of the cold weather and hot water.

Besides keeping us and our clothes clean, Mother was faced with the soul-destroying task of feeding Dad and our growing family. There being no family allowance payments in those days, she was confronted each week with stretching out one person's wage. It was bad enough when he was earning, but in 1921 he was made redundant through the closure of his firm. Dad had been a tradesman apprentice from 16 years of age. His trade was now obselete. I remember him saying to me: 'Son, I've never known it so bad. I have lost my job, our savings are gone, I can't get another employment and we're right on the floor.' Then my mother, God bless her, would smile and say: 'Don't let it get you down, things will buck up, that's for sure.' But she was wrong. Things didn't get better—they got a great deal worse and for the next few years we had to depend on charity: the Lord Mayor's Christmas Fund and the Board of Guardians.

How my mother managed, to this day I do not know. There was only one time that I remember when she seemd defeated. On coming home from school one midday, I found her crying. The previous day, Dad had appeared before the Board of Guardians. This board mostly comprised of well-to-do citizens called 'Guardians of the Poor'. Appointed by the government, they were empowered to cross examine all applicants to find out if they were the deserving poor—and not scrounging. Apparently a well-known female Guardian had said: 'You have a large family haven't you? Why not try boiling up potato peelings, I am advised they make a nourishing soup.' In reply my Dad, calmly and dispassionately said: 'It might suit you, a big fat sow, but not my children.' He was refused benefits until he apologised. We had no money to buy food. I went straight out and, off a delivery cart, pinched a loaf of bread and half a pound of butter.

That afternoon at Emmanuel School, St Philips, I worried, not so much about committing the sin of stealing, but about how Mum was going to manage. I decided to confess it all to my headmaster, Old Tomlins.

Our headmaster was, physically, an enormous man, standing about six feet tall and weighing around 16 stone. He was a strict disciplinarian, brooking no transgression of the rules. I'd sensed, however, that beneath that hard exterior there existed another person. Despite this, I approached him with some trepidation. He heard my story quietly. Then he said: 'You know what would have happened if you had been caught, eh? It would have been the reformatory school for you.' I burst out crying and said 'I would do it again, don't you understand? My mother was upset, and had nothing to feed us with.' He sent me away. Just before school ended he called me to his room and put an envelope in my hand and in a gruff voice said: 'You are a good lad. Don't do it again, but see me first, won't you?' I ran all the way home, and handed the envelope to my mother. It contained two pound notes. In the meantime, the neighbours had heard of Dad's clash with the hated enemy, and a parcel of groceries was collected from people who had so little to spare themselves.

Yes, there were hard days. St Philips was a slum, but there was more compassion and good in its squalid streets, and more saints living and working there, than in the whole of Rome.

Christmas 1918

Danny Price

It was approaching Christmas, 1918. The boy had not spent this day with his Dad since 1913. He was now seven.

As each day came, in response to his restless enquiries, Mum would say: 'He'll soon be home, this time for good.'

On Christmas Eve, for the umpteenth time: 'Mum, when's Dad coming?' She looked at him with a resigned look and replied: 'You go and buy your present for Dad and we'll both say a little prayer. Let us have faith.'

Therefore, on the eve of Christmas Day, a little boy was to be seen mingling with the crowds in Old Market Street, Bristol. The tramcars were disgorging happy smiling throngs at the entrance to Castle Street, which was a sparkling fairy grotto through which a mass of gay, joyous humanity poured. No traffic could possibly penetrate this seething conglomeration. The boy stood, transfixed by the scene of lights, movement and sound. People had come to live, celebrate and spend after four years of death and destruction.

The boy had a bright shilling clutched tightly in his fist. This was for a present for his Dad. What could he buy? He turned into the gaily lit bazaar and stood listening to a girl playing a piano, singing and selling popular sheet music. She was singing 'I'm forever blowing bubbles'. As the crowd around her scrambled forward for the penny sheets for the song he turned away, humming the chorus and then, suddenly, he knew the present he wanted. A pipe. Why hadn't he thought of it before? It was the mental image of 'Bubbles' and something his teacher had said in class about the nations sitting down to smoke the pipe of peace. Now, where could he get this pipe?

He ambled through Castle Street, that romantic thoroughfare Mary-le-Port Street, the fruit market, looking in every shop, but could find nothing to suit his taste and especially his pocket.

Outside a pub near the market, called The Rummer, he noticed three older boys singing carols. He stopped idly, watching and then he heard one of them say: 'Look at that little 'un. Gosh! I'll bet with that innocent face and blonde curly hair he'd collect piles of money.' The others agreed and he was invited to join them, but remembering his errand he raced away.

At the top of High Street, under the clock where the two figures of men strike with their hammers as time passes, he saw in a tobacconist's shop window just what he had been looking for. A dark brown curly pipe. He could picture his Dad puffing contentedly as he sat in front of the fire telling stories of his battles with the Hun.

There was no price on it. He dashed excitedly into the shop. 'How much is that pipe, Mister?' The grey haired man took it from the window. 'That'll cost you ten shillings' he replied. The boy's face dropped. How could he possibly obtain a further nine shillings? His mind then flashed back to the invitation outside the pub, to join the boys in their carol singing. 'Mister, can you keep this pipe for me? I'll pay this bob as a deposit.' The shopkeeper looked at the appealing face and agreed.

Above: Old Market Street in its heyday. (Photograph: Reece Winstone Collection)

Below: The author's father (standing) in 1914.

The boy dashed back to where he had last seen the carollers, but despite an intensive search could find no trace of them. He found himself outside The Grotto pub. Peeping inside when the door opened he could see the noisy, smoky, crowded interior packed with people, many still in uniform. Should he try by himself? He bucked up courage and raised his voice. 'While shepherds watched their flocks by night . . .' It is doubtful whether anyone inside heard anything. He opened the door and was immediately knocked flying to the floor by a number of soldiers entering the pub. He was picked up by a big, red-faced sergeant. 'Say, what's a little fella like you doing in a place like this?' The boy struggled out of his arms and with a sob in his throat said: 'My Daddy has been in hospital in France and I'm singing carols 'cos I wants to buy 'im a Christmas present for 'is coming home for Christmas.' The sergeant picked him up and he and the rest of the soldiers cleared the way through the crowds and stood him on the counter in the bar. Then, in a loud voice heard on many a barrack square, he said: 'Listen, everyone, to this little boy who wants to sing for his Dad, a soldier in hospital. He wants to buy him a present.' He turned. 'Sing laddie.' The boy instinctively knew this was a golden opportunity, and in his strong clear voice he sang 'Silent Night'. He put everything into it and, as the last notes rang out, there was a brief, painful silence. The sergeant's hat, when passed around, was full of money. The boy thanked him and dashed back to the shop.

Entering, he placed a grubby handkerchief in which the money was wrapped on the counter. ' 'Ere you are, Mister, have I got enough for that pipe?' Un-beknown to him, the shop was not empty. A quiet elderly man was in the corner looking at some brands of tobacco and could hear everything. The shopkeeper looked at the boy, a dirty little urchin, and then coldly and suspiciously asked: 'Where did you get this money, eh?' Puzzled, the boy looked up, and then the significance behind the question struck him. 'Look 'ere, Mister, I didn't pinch it.' He then burst out, recounting the whole story. The stranger heard it all. Approaching, he said: 'I couldn't help overhearing this little lad's story, so if you haven't enough, I will pay the balance.' The cash was counted. It was 1/3d short. The difference was paid by the stranger who said: 'Now, sonny, I'd like to join you in giving your soldier daddy a Christmas present and so I am enclosing in the parcel a supply of tobacco.' He paused then put his hand in his inner pocket, to pull out a shiny gold watch. With tears in his eyes, he handed it to the boy, saying: 'This belonged to my son, who last year was killed in action on the Western Front. You have it, laddie, he would like that.' He turned: 'Good luck to all your family and merry Christmas.' And he left.

The boy hurried home. Dad had not arrived. Crestfallen he went to bed, listening to the late night worshippers going to midnight service.

At one minute to twelve he heard the organ in the church strike up 'Oh Come All Ye Faithful'. This was accompanied by a loud knocking at the door. He rushed downstairs, to see his mother opening the door to a broken figure. With tears in his eyes he ran to the outstretched arms. 'Merry Christmas, Dad.'

Every time I pull out my watch, I remember saying those words, over seventy years ago, as clearly as if it all happened yesterday.

Clifton in the 'Twenties

Cynthia Floyd

Some of my earliest memories are of visiting my grandmother when she was caretaker to the Clifton, Bristol & Counties Ladies' Club at 45, Royal York Crescent. The National Council of Women of Great Britain & Ireland also used the address.

Running ahead of my mother, I could recognise the house by its luxuriant covering of wisteria. The profusion of blossom had merited a large photograph in the local press.

The main public room of the club was at balcony level. This was elegantly furnished and strewn with the many glossy society magazines of those days. A large globe, centrally placed, was possibly an indication of more serious interests. My grandmother had a kitchen in the basement and a sitting-room to which she had brought some of her own furniture. Her bedroom was on an upper floor. Miss Emily Harriet Smith J.P., one of the club's joint hon. secs., sometimes asked us to join her in the balcony room and I would become absorbed in the panoramic view over the Cumberland Basin and the Avon to the green hills beyond.

An incident reminds me that the house was still, in the 'twenties, lit by gas. We had just finished tea, one winter afternoon, and were basking in the heat from the kitchen range. As it began to grow dark, my grandmother lit a wax taper and invited me, as a special treat, to accompany her. Up through the house we climbed—and number 45 is a storey higher than the adjoining properties—pausing on each landing to light the gas and leave it burning low. How mysteriously shadowy the stair well seemed to a young child!

By 1929, owing perhaps to changing economic and social conditions, the club was no more. My grandmother then became housekeeper to Miss Smith and her sister Miss Sophia T. Smith, at their home, Richmond House, on Clifton Hill.

When visiting her there, we entered by a door in Clifton Road. The housekeeper's narrow sitting-room, leading off the kitchen, had a high shuttered window overlooking the paved path still to be seen through the tall iron gates. Tea would be brought in by one of the maids and while the grown-ups chatted I would be content to examine my grandmother's many ornaments and pictures, chief among them being a portrait of her first sweetheart. Occasionally I was permitted to explore the garden, where a path set with pebbles led to a gloomy summerhouse. Once, when the Misses Smith were away, we went into the dark, heavily-furnished dining-room. At either end of a sideboard was the hoof and foreleg of a horse, embellished with an engraved silver plate. These were relics of the Misses Smiths' favourite mounts from the riding days of their girlhood.

When, after only a year or two, my grandmother retired from this post, her employers awarded her a pension of ten shillings a week. This was considered most unusual in the circumstances and proof of the high regard in which she was held.

Although of humble origin and with little or no formal education, my

The author's grandmother, Mrs Annie Floyd, with her younger son, Clarence, and his wife, Doris, elder daughter of the Westcott family of the Richmond Springs, Gordon Road.

grandmother could, herself, have passed for one of these Clifton gentlewomen. Tall and stately, she made her own clothes, often of richly-coloured brocade or velvet and having beads of jet sewn about them. Her skirts were ankle-length, then quite usual for older women. Her abundant white hair was coiled at the back of her head and surmounted by a majestic hat. Massinghams of Princess Victoria Street fitted her long, narrow feet with Sir Herbert Barker shoes, over which she wore spats. She was ready to rally one, in any of life's little exigences, with an apposite line or two from the Poets.

In years long past, she had been engaged to a carpet firm's export representative. Visiting a cannibal chief, on his last voyage before their wedding, he contracted a fatal dose of fever and his body was consigned to the waves off the West Coast of Africa. This young man was always afterwards spoken of with reverence and seems to have been remarkable for nobility and sweetness of character, like a true Victorian hero. In time she married his friend, a Civil Servant, and being widowed at a fairly early age took up domestic work where, making use of various skills, including carpentry and upholstery, she seemed content.

Of course, a housekeeper was not expected to run a large house without assistance, when buckets of coal and cans of hot water still had to be carried up many stairs and much dusting and polishing of heavy furniture was required. Maidservants abounded in the Clifton of the 'twenties and were augmented by charwomen who came in to do 'the rough'—the scrubbing of stone floors and passages and other heavy work. My grandmother did not patronize domestic agencies but preferred to recruit girls from the Welsh mining valley of her childhood. Most of these fourteen-year-olds had never left home before, so their parents were glad for them to be given work under her supervision and she found places for girls in several Clifton households. These Welsh girls all addressed my grandmother as 'Auntie' and were devoted to her until her death, keeping in touch with her family for many years afterwards.

One little maid, Becca, was somewhat retarded. Her great pleasure was to be continually occupied with household chores. I remember the fascination with which, at six years of age, I gazed at a small area of linoleum beneath the kitchen window which Becca would insist on polishing over and over again unless provided with an alternative task. As a girl in her native village, poor Becca had been seduced. The daughter who resulted became in due course maid to the Westcott family at the Richmond Springs in nearby Gordon Road and was generally understood to be Becca's niece. Even my mother was not allowed to know during my grandmother's lifetime that the girl was really Becca's daughter. Once when we visited Richmond House, Becca's father, a devout Welsh non-conformist, was being entertained in the kitchen. The old man had apparently been quite broken down by his daughter's shame.

Towards the end of the decade, changes were becoming evident in Clifton. One afternoon my grandmother took me for a stroll along York Place and there below us, where the ground fell away down the hillside, we saw a great building site alive with toiling workmen. In impressive tones, she charged me to remember in years to come that I had witnessed the building of the residence for women students to be known as Manor Hall. Little could she have anticipated that the house where she was living was destined for the same use.

Rosie

Cynthia Floyd

Kingsley Road is situated behind Cheltenham Road, below Cotham Brow. Although containing only eighteen houses, it has a flavour of its own. With one exception, the houses are Victorian. They are pleasantly varied in design but most have a flight of steps leading up to a dignified front door. All are dominated by the railway arch that spans the road about half-way along.

The line is carried on either side by further arches, the viaduct being constructed from great rough-hewn blocks of stone. Near the 'bus stop it is grown over with ivy and gives the impression of a natural cliff rising from the unkempt grass of the steep bank. Just below this bank is the single house of a later date. An obvious example of in-filling, it yet seems solitary and the french windows spread across its frontage are closely curtained. Leaving the 'bus on a winter evening, one can imagine it the setting of a pre-war detective story but when a train passes overhead against a summer sky, on its way through the Avon Gorge to the tiny run-down resort of Severn Beach, the scene speaks only of romance. An unusual road, then, and for some years it could even have been considered unique.

My mother, who was born in the closing years of the last century, remembers visiting Tudor Villa, number twelve, as a child. It was a family home, several big brothers having a pretty golden-haired little sister called Rosie. Many years later, Mother returned as an old lady to live at the top of the hill. Often she would walk down to the shops, returning on the half-hourly 'bus. She soon noticed the immaculate state of Kingsley Road. No 'bus ticket, confectionery wrapping or dead leaf was allowed to remain in evidence for many minutes. She noticed, moreover, the neat little stooped figure with dustpan and brush who, all through the day and in any weather, patrolled the road with eyes only for litter. This, she realised, was Rosie. A Rosie too absorbed in her self-imposed task to recognize neighbour or passer-by, let alone an aquaintance from a distant childhood. There, for all to appreciate, was the quite surprising difference made when a city street is completely litter-free.

The background remains; the little train still passes overhead; the only obvious change is underfoot. The road is now like any other. Drink cans and take-away food containers, drifts of decaying leaves in season, 'bus tickets and other ephemera await the attention that can be afforded by Corporation road sweepers. There is no successor to Rosie.

Was she motivated by the lonely eccentricity of advancing years or did she truly love and wish to care for the road where she was living out her quiet life? It is several years since she departed, so we shall probably never know.

Remembered Road

Cynthia Floyd

To my mother, Sefton Park Road appears little changed since she lived there early in the century. The long lines of plane trees, interspersed with a few limes, still survive to relieve the monotony of the hundred and fifty-seven late Victorian houses. She finds the most noticeable difference to be the influx of cars. In her recollection, however, the road was far from quiet and deserted without them.

For a start there were hoofbeats. The housewife had little need to visit the shops if she was not so inclined, for tradesmen made regular deliveries of all day-to-day necessities, usually by means of a horse and cart. The horses knew the routes they had to follow and the various stopping places involved. They also knew where they could expect a little friend to come running with a lump of sugar. Then there were the errand boys, cycling to and fro with specific orders. Famed for their cheerful whistling, they always managed to include the latest tune in their repertoires.

In addition to ordinary household requirements, more exotic commodities were brought round. Once a week, Miss Chambers came driving in from the country with home-made brawn. For Dada and Mama this delicacy made a tasty supper but none of the children would touch it, objecting that it was 'hairy'. Easter brought the cry of, 'One a penny, two a penny, Hot Cross Buns!' Later the Welsh cockle-woman, her wares in a tub balanced on her head, made a colourful picture. Occasional visitors were the umbrella mender, the knife and scissors grinder and the gipsy who offered a selection of haberdashery, fascinating to a little girl. When the aspidistra seller trundled his handcart along the road there was no need to worry about the housekeeping money. Flourishing plants could be had in exchange for jam jars! Another trader who accepted jars as payment was the balloon man. He arrived on Saturday morning when the children were at home, his cart a multi-coloured splendour.

In contrast to the traders, there were those who offered entertainment. The organ-grinder with his smartly attired, pathetic little monkey was eagerly awaited and could be induced by an extra coin to delay his departure. Sometimes a Scottish piper in all his finery proceeded majestically by, but the most memorable musical treat came on a Friday evening. This was the visit of the harpist. While a frail old man went from door to door collecting, the harpist, a strangely remote figure and always heavily veiled, would draw from the harp tones of such beauty that the children could easily imagine this to be veritable music of heaven. Although they loved to dance and sing to the music of the organ-grinder, their response to the harp was one of rapt attention. As the two sombre figures pushed the heavy instrument away, an atmosphere of deep tranquility seemed to linger in the gathering dusk.

Just as entertainment was provided, so too was a news service. Anything at all sensational would call for a special edition of the local newspaper and the unintelligible cries of the barefoot newsboys would be heard. The price was a halfpenny but my mother was to remember that Dada always gave a whole

16

penny and never waited for change.

Of course this life of the street was common to all parts of the city. In one respect, however, the road where Mother lived was different. It backed on to the grounds of the group of five great orphanages built by Mr George Müller. Sometimes crocodiles of orphans would pass the house, the girls quaintly dressed in long print dresses, straw bonnets and shawls. Beyond the back garden, orphan boys could be seen tending the extensive vegetable plots and by six o'clock in the morning large uncurtained windows revealed them hard at work scrubbing floors. The orphans all looked well fed and cared for, but the children did not envy them their regimented life and were, perhaps, more appreciative of their own good fortune.

Today, when the need to provide for such large numbers of children has fortunately passed, the work continues in other ways and the former orphanages house a technical college. For those living in the long road, however, the buildings still stand as a memorial to the results achieved through George Müller's trust in the faithfulness of God.

Playground with School Attached

Henry Belcher

In 1930 Downend was in Gloucestershire the wrong side, some would say, of the Bristol boundary. Avon sounds urban but schoolboys the world over will agree is easier to spell.

In those days we supported five pubs, had a forge, a cricket field, a fine old parish church and a mixed school. The term 'the poor' was deeply fashionable, the elderly and the infirm feared the workhouse and those who had to sign on went to Kingswood Labour Exchange. Our member of Parliament was Sir Derek Gunston but I don't think he ever came to Downend.

The village green, that open space near the church, became the school playground. The Victorian developers moved in to build their classrooms next to it using a local reddish grey stone and a lime mortar cement the colour of sour milk.

We lived in Salisbury Road, our house one of a run-down rank of five. We had two rooms up and two down plus a damp, dark, cold, back kitchen. Grandad lived with us and like my dad (in 1930 language) 'belonged to the Salvation Army'. These kinsfolk of mine believed in freedom—by abstension—from drunkenness, tobacco and gambling. (Sounds ludicrous for they had no money for any of those things!)

Downend Church of England Boys' (apostrophe after the ess) School was but an Olympic javelin's throw from home, near enough for us ten year olds to kick a tennis ball to school, hurry home at dinnertime then kick it back again. When we arrived the crowded playground took over.

The good red soil of South Gloucestershire, pounded hard by booted generations before us, formed the playground surface. Hard on schoolboy knees yet eminently suitable for marbles and hopscotch for the girls. North Street was unfenced but to the north was a formidable house wall over which no ball ever went. On the west side a slightly drunken churchyard wall mercifully kept in check the mounds of neglected graves from spilling over into our precious play area.

Playground activity was intense, the girls and their skipping ropes taking early refuge on the public pathway to the south for in 1930 they were happy to be driven rather than drive. That spoil-sport, the bellringer crept up on us unseen, ringing her bell passionately as though her life depended upon it. Readin', writin', rithmetic. Readin', writin', rithmetic, the bell clanged again, again and again.

We well knew of the skills on offer, chalk and cheese different, yet complementary to lessons learned from playground fraternisation. But why did she go on so long?

I feared the threatened embarrassment of those random 'dirty head' flea inspections organised by the District Nurse and carried out immediately after morning bell. We were press-ganged into a queue, soon learned she looked for flea bites around the neck. If she found any she would 'go to town' on the victim with her super fine tooth comb. I can't honestly say I saw her stamp on any fleas that fell from it but sadly it was the same boys singled out each time. The whispered conversation between her and the invigilating teacher added to their humiliation.

Blackboards and easels were in daily use, our teachers constantly juddering this top-heavy apparatus into position. Silently we watched, shared their grimaces, never daring to warn. The teaching technique was 'chalk (white) and talk', the blackboard an early day computer with a one-day memory bank.

Facts, fiction and trivia loitered in chalk before our eyes. Books to read, Kings of England, doing word verbs, adjectives, vulgar fractions, decimals. At the end of the day the cleaning ritual ensured nothing would be remembered except perhaps vital historical dates like 1066.

Mr Perkins, our kindly headmaster, caned me twice. With a tinge of emotion he breathed his pre-punishment apology. 'This is going to hurt me more than it hurts you'. His bamboo had lengthwise splits that increased the whip, the swish and the pain.

I wasn't aware of the existence of a punishment record book or if there was, what questions the columns might ask. Cane replacement would constitute for him a problem of conscience—not easily resolved.

One fine pre-Christmas morning, the early birds discovered a huge packing-case astride the school entrance, the labels of which bore the imprint 'The Great Western Railway'. It proved to be a gift container of cornflakes, one packet apiece for each pupil. We learned the donor was an ex-school-boy of ours named Brown who had emigrated to Canada and had made good with the Kellogg Cornflake Company. I've been eating them ever since.

Insecurity was part of our elementary education. Suddenly school uniforms were the order of the day, navy blue gym-slips for the girls, caps with red and green segments for the boys. I never did learn how much they cost—my parents did not have the money. Shortly after I was taken into the dark confines of the cloakroom where I tried on several, finally going home with a nearly-new one which had a luxurious fawn lining. I hope I said 'Thank you'.

Resuming lessons after lunch was vexing. Uncomfortably hot and dishevelled we trooped in to breathlessly answer the register, digging deep into our pockets for handkerchiefs we knew we never had. Empire Day was the one exception. With scrubbed faces and clean shirts the entire school assembled on the playground beneath (almost) the flag of St George fluttering high up on the church tower.

Ignoring the graves, old and new, we crunched along the winding gravel pathway into church. Window-width shafts of sunlight cut through the gloom; up front the vicar looked approvingly on his sidesmen as they ferried hymn books and guided us to our seats.

We sniffed at the reflected smell of age-old C of E timbers, of Bath sandstone and pew varnish. It was warm, someone yawned disrespectfully and a teacher moved quickly to stop the rot. With the others I sat on the hard pew, felt like an intruder. Nor was the soft hassock my toes located mine, but the hymn was, for sing I could and sing I must.

Houses in Salisbury Road, Downend. The author spent his first twenty five years in the end house, photographed during the Second World War. The Belchers paid a rent of 6/8d a week. The family air raid shelter can just be seen in the picture. For wartime, their neighbours' clear strip of garden is puzzling.

'Summer suns are glowing over land and sea
Happy light is flowing bountiful and free'

We never suspected hostile forces were gathering with greedy eyes on this empire, that two of our number, Douglas Wise, Royal Navy and George Evans, Merchant Navy, would shortly have their names forever engraved in war memorial stone.

Leaving the church gloom we filed back to the playground sunshine to be dismissed. Some of the afternoon and all of this springtime evening was ours.

Our schoolboy love affair with the playground was promiscuous, rarely did we linger after school, never sent a card during those long summer holidays. But we loved it all the same. It hated silence, was allergic to summer litter, shrugged off dirty winter slush, saved for us crisp snowball snow. It was sympathetic to the schoolboy plots hatched there, for those bent on administration it was their very first board room. When the autumn winds swept the leaves under the cemetery wall we let them be. Only the ruffians amongst us dared to disturb their soft contours.

Headmasters come and go but our playground, unsung, has maintained an unbroken record of service to education, long before and since my day. Now it is tarmacked over, fenced in by pre-fabricated classrooms and a canteen. Iron railings painted black protect the children.

Astride the gate at breaktime a teacher bellringer, her empty coffee mug beside her, holds sway. I'm not sure if her bell is our bell.

20

Hotwells remembered

Albert McGrath

Gran said to me, 'Come on Bert, we're going up the fish market', and I knew what to do. I crossed over the front room that was our flat in the Lebec tenement house in Dowry Parade, and switched on our Cossor wireless. The set took some time to warm up but eventually the station sounded and I switched to between it and the other stations until I got the 'mush' of the aerial station and turned up the volume.

It was all Gran McGrath's idea. Soon, in the background of the 'mush' she heard 'it', a definite burr-burr-burr . . . and growing stronger all the time. Then, as it grew in strength, it became a humming-like whine . . . 'Come on, Bert, get your coat on and switch off' . . . we both left the Lebec and hurried to the tram-stop . . . just as the clanking, heaving, swaying tram rounded the corner by Lady Haberfield's almshouses. The heavy thick wires overhead had done their other job—they'd told Gran just how near off the tram was—even to the very precise comment: 'Ees just passin' Freeland Place' . . . it *never* failed.

Hotwells, for me, holds many memories. Unemployment, there, as everywhere, was rampant. Kids wore jumble-boots, left offs, sacking trousers (long trousers)—mine were out of an old sugar bag with the words 'Tate & Lyle' across the knees, stitching, by Gran, again, in string. Then there were the Lord Mayor's Christmas Dinner Boots to take us through mashy winters, much to the sadistic delight of people like Winnie who mocked us by crying delightedly, 'oo look, they've got the Lord Mayor's boots on' . . . her identification was made easier by the huge tags on each pair.

Fleas, bugs and cockroaches were but a few of our constant companions in the Lebec, as were diphtheria, scarlet fever and even tuberculosis . . . it was nothing rare to see the fever van draw up to a house and a child wrapped in a scarlet blanket carried out and rushed away to the Fever Hospital (Ham Green).

Death often came into our midst. Young Donald was killed in the cattle 'lairs' behind the Bonds on the riverbank. They used to play 'chicken' to run past the heavy-sided cattle vans and pull the retaining pins and poor Don caught the end of the bolt in the temple. 'Ginger' was taken out of the lock basin—white and swollen, and very dead—Mr M. was knocked down and killed, to lie in the little side room of their flat for a whole week. We, as kids, were somewhat terrified at the thought of the body in the coffin *upstairs* . . .

Gran used to say to me, 'Bert, run over and get me a half a pint of stout from the Dowry. When I returned with it in the white jug, I'd stand fascinated as she slowly put a red hot poker into its middle. She explained: 'it'll warm the cockles of me 'eart'.

Faggots and peas and mash from way-off Redcliffe Hill were always sought for—the distance presented no problem, as people walked in those days. The tuppeny rush at the Hotwells 'bughouse' cinema was another part of sheer neighbourhood delight, but all enjoying themselves to the hilt.

Love Street, Hotwells in the 1920s. (Photograph: Reece Winstone Collection)

Speedway boat racing on the Avon brought me the first half crown I'd ever seen. The man said, 'here you kiddo, this is for looking after my van' . . . I ran the half mile home in record breaking time. Gran, shrewd as ever, said 'I'll look after two bob of it, you have the sixpence'. I didn't care, I took it—to Fanny Brown's shop in Hope Chapel Hill where I bought loads upon loads of sherbert, locust-beans, dolly mixtures and bulls-eyes . . .

One night I lay under the stars in the Western Desert on my groundsheet bed and cried with unstoppable nostalgia for my Hotwells and the youthful days of happiness.

. . . and off to the 'Pro'

Albert McGrath

School—the real school, as we old 'uns say—was a very, very hardly ever missed thing. Although diphtheria and other childhood diseases of those days raged throughout the land, most children, if unaffected, went to school. We went, as per our strict parents, to *learn* . . . as my Gran used to say (in her age-old wisdom) 'to become trees that grow, not planks'.

My main schooling was at the Pro-Cathedral School in Park Place in Clifton. I lived in Hotwells, and that meant something like a mile and a half there—and then back, making roughly three miles a day. *We walked*. It often seemed we were, in a sense, going on a safari . . . Hope Chapel Hill . . . North Green Street . . . The Polygon . . . part of Cornwallis Avenue . . .

Hensman's Hill . . . Meridian Place . . . arriving at the 'Pro' about a quarter to nine. If we 'put our skates on' it was no spooky, interrupted journey, although the Polygon in the deep winter was rather frightening. We—my sister and I—would literally hurl ourselves through its length by shouting out conversations such as (me) 'Come on, Eileen, we'll be late'. She would reply, 'I'm going as fast as I can, Bert,' and one could almost hear our two hearts thumping as we passed through the dreaded Polygon, narrow and very badly lit. Secretly, I always thought Jack the Ripper must be waiting there . . . emerging into Cornwallis Avenue we showed our relief by glowing expressions of high delight on our faces.

The 'Pro' was a Catholic School, next to the wonderful Cathedral itself. I still remember lots of the very excellent teachers I grew to like, and although some nearly sixty years have passed, their attempts to teach us savages the arts of civilisation. In those days, the cane was very much in evidence. It was dreaded, I can tell you. It had almost the same type of shock as seeing the Judge with his black cap on—seeing the teacher about to apply hand-caning and listening to that absurd nonsense about 'this is going to hurt me more that it hurts you' . . .

I kept away from the cane as much as possible. It *was* a deterrent, most definitely. One day I told a bigger boy that 'they cannot give you more than *four*—two on each hand'. Unfortunately, he in turn told his pet teacher what I had said . . . and although I had only qualified for four cuts of the cane, I actually got six. Our teachers included several nuns. My favourites were Sister Coleman and Sister Maria. My dislike of the religion was the 'Sunday' roll-call. On Monday, the priest would enter with his mass book and call out each pupil's name. When he came to mine it was usually 'Nine o'clock Mass' . . . not (like the others) Nine o'clock Mass, catechism *and* benediction . . . which often made the priest add 'Very, very good' . . . and I got lower in my seat feeling I needed a 'holy' kind of wash to bring my religious status up to the others' level.

I remember one particular question we answered in our Catechism books. 'Is the Pope infallible?' It wasn't the content of the question, it was the word 'infallible' that stuck with me all my life. I remember some years ago telling an antagonist in a public debate, 'You're not infallible, you're not the Pope of Rome', and that's how the good teachings of Park Place stuck, like the two-times-two tables and the excellent school meals dished up by 'Ma' Spencer and her daughter May. Cocoa, and bread and cheese, potato soup and thick creamy rice pudding.

We played rough in the playground, but no beltings, no kicking. Indeed, we played joyfully but not injuriously—and (this is true enough) we didn't sit poised to hear the bell tolling the end of school for that day.

Our journey home was a thing of sheer delight. We took the longer route of Clifton Vale—mainly so that we could see into the windows of Ted Davis' and Harry Evans' shops—and ended up with Gran saying, 'Come on, here's your tea', part of which was a hefty slice of the brilliant cake she'd so expertly cooked, full of currants and sultanas. Then, no rushing out into the beyond—washing the tea things was of the highest importance. Then errands. *Then* play. Life was indeed hard, but happy.

Bristol in the 1930s

Angela Tippetts

Clattering up the steps to ride on top of a Bristol tramcar is now only a memory, but for a child in the 1930s it was by far the best way to travel. The open top of the tramcar gave you a fine view of the city, and if you were lucky enough to sit in the front seat you could watch the driver turning his wheel as we clanked along. A ride to the end of the line meant that you could see the change round. The arm that connected with the overhead wires was swung round and reconnected for the return journey. Both ends of the tramcar being the same the driver just walked to the other end to drive back. The Tramway Centre with its triangle surrounded by tramcars, and large ships right in the heart of the city when the river came up as far as Baldwin Street, are now but a distant memory.

I recall the lamplighter cycling from lamp post to lamp post at dusk every day. His long pole reached to the top of the pillar and switched on each light. In the mornings he returned to put them all out again.

Who could forget the 'Stop Me and Buy One' man tinkling the bell of his ice cream tricycle, with the tubs, bricks and Snofruits in their blue and white check wrappers in the ice box in front. 'Can we have one please?' we would cry, and rush out to catch him before he vanished.

'Special, special extra, late news, read all about it' was the cry of the newspaper boys, and we would be sent out to buy a paper wondering what the extra news was all about. In the mid thirties there were plenty of special items with the death of King George V, the abdication of the Prince of Wales, first rumoured and then confirmed, and the accession of King George VI. I still have the Coronation mugs which all the schoolchildren were given—one for the coronation of King Edward VIII, which never took place, and the other for the coronation of King George VI and Queen Elizabeth, which did take place.

The cinema was in its heyday and on Saturday mornings we children, clutching our pennies, queued outside the Whiteladies Cinema in Whiteladies Road. Inside was a magical world where we cheered our heroes and booed their enemies. I saw all Shirley Temple's films on a Saturday morning at the Whiteladies.

On Saturday afternoons we went to Castle Street, to Woolworth's, and Peacock's 1d Bazaar. 'Nothing over 6d' (now 2½p) was Woolworth's slogan, and I still use a pocket encyclopaedia which I bought for that sum in the 1930s. Castle Street was always thronged with cheerful people walking in the road as well as on the pavements, making it impossible for cars to drive through the mass of people. Sometimes we had to go to Wine Street where the fascinating Dutch House stood on the corner, or to Bridge Street where

(Photograph: Reece Winstone)

25

the Scholastic had the corner site, but none of the other streets compared to Castle Street which had an atmosphere all its own. The shops stayed open until late at night and many a housewife waited till the last minute to buy the Sunday roast when prices were reduced. There were no fridges in those days and perishable goods were sold off for a song on Saturday nights. In Peter Street which led into Castle Street was the News Theatre where, the shopping done, we would sink into a seat to see Mickey Mouse and his gang as well as the Pathé News. Castle Street was an enchanted place where you could buy everything. How sad that it has gone, nothing could ever replace it.

Everyone wore hats in those days, and we children wore velours in the winter and panamas in the summer. Winter also meant much loathed black woollen stockings kept up with garters, and liberty bodices.

On Good Friday the bakers' boys would tour the streets crying 'Hot Cross Buns', and we would buy them fresh and spicy from their baskets.

In the summer there were picnics under the May trees on Durdham Downs, at Blaise Castle, or Charlton Common, sadly destroyed for the Brabazon runway which was never used.

I went to school at St. John's at the top of the Blackboy, and remember playing rounders on the Downs, and walking in crocodile down Blackboy Hill to St John's Church on Ash Wednesday and Ascension Day.

November 5th was an exciting day, there was always a huge bonfire on the Downs at the top of Blackboy Hill. We visited this but were rather scared of the fireworks which the older boys threw into the crowd. Our great joy was the firework display which took place every year at Bristol Zoo, when we stood on the Downs opposite the Zoo to watch the set pieces. The animals were all shut up before the fireworks started.

Armistice Day on November 11th was kept by everyone, whichever day of the week it fell on. At 11 o'clock cars stopped, people in the streets or at work stood still, and there was a great hush over everything while the two minutes' silence was kept. This created a big impression on a child, and perhaps it is a pity it died out. It gave us a sense of patriotism which doesn't exist today.

Christmas meant the pantomime at the Princes Theatre in Park Row, lavish spectacles looked forward to eagerly. I recall the smell of perfume which always wafted around the theatre. The Princes was destroyed by bombs in the 1940s, and no other pantomimes ever compared with those we had seen there.

Flags and decorations seemed to feature often in the 1930s. The main streets had flags and bunting strung across them on all special occasions such as Royal events and Brighton Week. When Royalty visited the city they always rode in horse drawn open carriages, and the schoolchildren lining the route and waving their Union Jacks had a clear view of them. They didn't walk about, of course, but I clearly remember seeing King George V and Queen Mary, and also the Prince of Wales.

They were happy days for a child in the 30s. 1939 brought not only the end of a decade but the end of a way of life.

Adventure playground

Joan Coombs

I was a deprived child in the thirties, but I didn't notice it—all the other children were deprived too! We all wore the Lord Mayor's shoes, had free dinners and milk and we all played with whatever was available. I cannot remember ever being anything but happy.

We were very fortunate in living in a district of Bristol that provided us with what might now be called Adventure Playgrounds, one of the best being Speedwell Pit Dumps and surrounding fields. We would climb the slag heaps, just as good, if not better, than Mount Everest. The lucky ones would ride up and down the smaller dumps on their ASP (all spare parts) bikes. We would climb the stunted trees that managed to grow between the mounds and as far as I was concerned we were on Mars with Flash Gordon, or galloping through Cowboyland with Buck Jones.

There was a large pool which we called Lily Pool. Can't remember any lilies but it was certainly abundant with wild life. Tadpoles, frogs, newts and even a few fish. I paddled there, not realising or caring about any diseases I might catch.

The fields adjoining were always referred to as 'The Gozzy'. In recent years I saw it described, much to my amazement, as 'a wooded valley'. It was full of blackberry bushes, and wild plum trees and a dirty little brook meandered through the bottom of it. The far end was used by the local pottery (long since defunct), as a dump for their waste. Since much of it consisted of chalk moulds we kids were well provided with chalk for our 'pottles' (a game of hopping from one number to the next) much to our mothers' annoyance. Many times I was made to wash the chalk marks from the pavements and had my chalk confiscated. They were more concerned with clean streets in those days.

There were also some old buildings which were in a very dangerous condition. I don't know what their original use was but some of it seemed to be brick kilns. We would crawl through them with no thought of danger, although I well remember becoming stuck in one once and the terror I felt when I could not move one way or the other. Perhaps that fear gave me extra impetus because I managed to wriggle out somehow.

A railway siding, with just one 'puffing billy' going backwards and forwards ran from the coal mine to the main railway. The sides of the track were covered with blackberry bushes and we would risk the wrath of the train driver to harvest them. We could hear the train coming easily, it made such a noise, and we would hide in the deepest part of the bushes, keeping perfectly still while it passed and then emerge to continue with our picking.

We would come home 'black as the ace of spades' as mother used to say, but tired and happy. I think the mothers were happy too, both to get rid of us for a while and to get the free fruit. I wonder if they would have been so happy had they known what danger we were in for at least some of the time!

The other place I remember very clearly is the towpath along the side of the River Avon, between Bristol and Hanham, now one of the outlying suburbs, but then 'the country'.

Down Troopers Hill, along Crews Hole past the tar works (have a sniff—it's good for bad colds) and so to the river. If we followed the road a short way we would come to a long flight of steps leading down to the towpath. The 'Hundred Steps', we called them. I never counted them but there were certainly quite a lot.

We had to pass a rubbish tip to get there and I was always fascinated by what must be in that tip and by the peculiar smell which emanated from it. Fear of getting 'the fever'—whatever that was—prevented me from going any farther than the gate, but there were often people there rummaging through the rubbish to see what they could find that was still usable. Some people were destitute and desperate in those days.

At the bottom of the steps there was a shallow bit of the river where we used to paddle. As long as you stayed near the bank you were safe. If you slid carefully round a rocky outcropping you could reach a spring which spouted its icy cold water into the river. We would drink from it and fill our water bottles. None of us ever contracted any terrible disease so presumably it was not polluted by any of the chemicals which contaminate such springs today.

Then off we would go, past Beese's Tea Gardens on the opposite side of the river and on to Hanham Woods and the Chequers Inn. If you had a penny you could use the ferry to get to the other side of the river and back. What an adventure! We looked with awe at Fry's Chocolate Factory and imagined all that chocolate in there, found a bird's nest and peeped in at the eggs and looked at a field covered with holes, which we decided was a rabbit warren.

Then, not realising that there was a bridge farther along which we could have used for nothing, we recrossed the ferry and retraced our steps, stopping only to pick bluebells in the woods to give to our mothers.

Deprived or not, I cannot say, all I know is that my memories of my childhood in Bristol are for the most part very good.

Riverside childhood

Gloria Reed

Walking about Hotwells recently on a quiet Sunday morning, intoxicated by sun and breeze, my sister and I approved the new houses and apartments by the riverside. We especially liked the modern cottages with seats outside their front doors facing the water, and contrasted them with many of the homes we knew when we were children.

My father, a local boy, grew up to return as minister of the Baptist Church at Hotwells, so most of our early years were spent in and around the district. It is difficult to imagine a happier childhood, for we were surrounded by our parents' families and many friends living in a close-knit community.

We didn't have a large country garden to play in. In fact at some of the places where we lived we had no garden at all to speak of, and we rarely went out to play in a street. If we went out we usually walked, or went to someone's house, and there was a considerable programme of church events. Anyway, who needed a big garden when we had all the joys of the waterfront, and a short stroll brought us to the Portway with its tiny park and Zigzag leading up to the Downs? Then there was Clifton, the Suspension Bridge and Leigh Woods to enjoy, Ashton Park not far away, and we were so near the Centre and the old-style College Green.

But most of all, of course, there was the river, which had a great effect on all our lives. Yes, rivers flow through other parts of the city, but ours was such a busy waterway, bustling with life and quick with activity, and we were quite familiar with big ships and small boats, and with people whose livelihood depended on the river. We would watch the smiling people returning on the white Campbell's steamers and the men who worked on the cargo ships that went through, and we learned the sounds of different engines and heard shouts in other languages whilst Great George, our timekeeper, struck the hours away.

My recollections of ships are most clear when I think of the years when we shared a home with Auntie Annie and Uncle Bill. They lived on the floors above P & O Campbell's offices in Britannia Buildings, right opposite Cumberland Basin. Uncle Bill had once worked for Campbell's and had gone with one of the steamers to pick up soldiers from a battlefield abroad.

They had a wide veranda which stretched over the 'shop' and there my uncle liked to sit, and much of our lives was filled with the sight of ships moving in and out of the Basin. It was one of our greatest pleasures and we recognised them, knew their names and their home ports, noted how regularly they came to our part of the world. Sometimes they went through at night, and we were disappointed not to see them but distinctly heard their engines and saw their moving lights as we lay in bed. We heard the foghorns boom when there was grey fog masking the banks. The hoots of the ships ushered out the Old Year and brought in the New as they answered one another in greeting.

Often we saw cattle being herded along the road. They went into the slaughterhouse and we smelled their strong odour. Another sight we loved

(Photograph: Port of Bristol Authority)

30

was that of a diver at work in the Basin, while another person on the bank wound the lifeline down. We always insisted on watching until he came up safely again.

One summer, I remember, Auntie Rose and I took a bicycle along the towpath by the bonded warehouses and tried to ride it, occasionally a train passing directly above us. We were happy to see trains running along on the other side of the river, and sometimes in summer we crossed to the station over there and went off for a day's outing.

Last January my sister and I went back with our husbands to celebrate her birthday within sight of the house where she was born. As we sat in the restaurant we remembered coming over to buy bread and hot cross buns nearby. The bridge was open to let a couple of ships pass through. It was like coming home.

When we were children our days were punctuated by the opening of the swing bridge, the queues of cars and lorries waiting to cross, the movement of the lock gates. Sometimes we were separated from our friends by the river, but the wait was never boring. If my brother and I were waiting when the barriers opened we tried to get on the bridge in time to feel the sensation of movement before it halted. We breathed sighs of enjoyment as we rode what could only have been a few inches, but this seemed thrilling to us.

Unfortunately the river sometimes tempted children to neglect safety, go too near the edge and fall in, and—sick at heart—we would hear that a boy in our Sunday School class or one who came to our church had drowned. Generally, however, we considered the river with respect and knew its dangers.

A few years later we moved to Southville and had to come to Hotwells most days. Sometimes we walked, though often we caught the ferry to the Mardyke. It didn't take long to cross the river, but we gazed into its depths with a little fear, although we also adored this mode of transport.

As the minister's children, church played a big part in our lives. Not only were there the services, but the social events too. We stood in the kitchen where ladies with aprons tied over their smart clothes cooked potatoes for suppers and used water from the big old-fashioned boiler for washing up, a fire burning merrily below. We rambled to Dundry Church tower or with our aunts and uncles and people from another chapel walked to Failand. Church was a place where we saw old friends, and made new ones.

When we renewed acquaintance with Hotwells after so many years, it was sad to find so many of the shops closed, so many friendly faces gone. We were startled to see the Baptist Church derelict, a windowless shell, humiliated and forlorn.

Hotwells is unique. From an early age we were aware of living close to history, for once the area was successful and sought after. In some houses we would see trim panelling and alcoves with curving shelves; there were terraces and balconies which told of wealth and taste. Like a once popular actress Hotwells grew old and forgotten when some of its charms faded. Then not so long ago it was remembered and rediscovered, to become successful and sought after once more. We hope it remains so.

Good Friday, 1941

Joyce Williams

I was making my way home from the office on that Good Friday afternoon when I noticed fire brigades from Gloucester and Cheltenham were driving into town, and as I turned into Cranbrook Road, the road in which I was then living, some mobile guns passed me, making their way to Redland Green, where they were often based. These activities did not unduly alarm me, as by the Spring of 1941, one had grown accustomed to such sights in Bristol.

I was working in the City Treasurer's office of Bristol Corporation, and had been sent down for a spell to the Rating Department which was temporarily situated in the Central Library, College Green, having been bombed out of the Corn Exchange. It was a bit of a tight squeeze, as we not only had to share accommodation with the Library Staff, but also with the Town Clerk's Department, which had suffered a similar fate. In 1940 the City Council decreed that all public offices should remain open on bank holidays (except Christmas Day) and that was the reason why I had spent the day in the office.

As soon as I arrived home, my mother had my evening meal awaiting me with her usual comment 'hurry up and eat it before they come', meaning the Germans. She could not bring herself to mention the word 'Germans' or 'Germany'.

We were washing up the dishes when the first bomb that night fell on a nearby road. We heard its whistle before the siren went, and did not have time to get to the Anderson shelter in the garden, so dived under the kitchen table away from the windows. It was one of the longest and most widespread air-raids we had experienced, with a short break around midnight. It was not until daylight that we heard the final 'all-clear'. Once again, we had no water, gas or electricity, but we had a coal fire in the breakfast room. Mother had somehow obtained a small hob, and attached it to a bar of the grate rather precariously, but we did manage to boil a kettle of water, or place a saucepan on it. From the first of the night time raids in the November, we had kept the bath, and as many buckets and utensils that we possessed, filled with water. It was a precious commodity in those days.

After breakfast, I started to make my way to the office, past burning buildings, rescue services still searching for people in the rubble, and seeing an occasional U.X.B. sign.

Scenes like this had become an all too familiar sight in 1940 and those early months of 1941. When I eventually reached the office, I discovered that although it had not received a direct hit, a bomb had fallen at the back of the building, on a grassy bank, and it had blown in the windows, together with much grass and earth. It had rained slightly for a short spell, and many of the files, papers and library books were covered with wet earth. As there seemed little inclination on the part of the citizens of Bristol to pay their rates on that Easter Saturday morning, staff helped to clear up. This was difficult, as there was no water, but we did manage to remove some of the dirt. What we desperately needed was a drink, but there was nothing to be had, the smoke from burning buildings nearby making us feel so thirsty.

During the morning, a rumour went around that Mr Churchill was at the University conferring degrees on important people. We could hardly believe it. However, when the office closed at 12.30pm a small group of girls, myself included, though extremely tired, made our way up the steep Park Street to the University. That famous shopping street had been badly damaged again, as had Queen's Road in which the University was situated. In fact, part of the University building had been on fire. Shops opposite were still burning, and firemen and A.R.P. personnel were busily engaged. Other than a couple of policemen on the steps of the University building, there was no sign to indicate that Mr Churchill was inside. A very small crowd had gathered, and eventually people started chanting 'we want Churchill'. Shortly afterwards, a group emerged from the building, led by Mr Churchill, and followed by Mr Winant, the American Ambassador, Mr Menzies, Prime Minister of New Zealand, upon whom Mr Churchill had been conferring degrees, Mr Avril Harriman, an American representative, the Lord Mayor, Sheriff, and University dignitaries. Many of the latter had their gowns over A.R.P. or Home Guard uniforms.

At first, Churchill looked over the little knot of people to the still burning buildings, and the scene of desolation all around, We in turn, gazed at this short stocky figure, whose radio speeches had so inspired us, despite his promise of blood, toil, sweat and tears, which had become such a reality. What was there about this man which so impressed us and gave us such confidence? I cannot, even nowadays, begin to explain.

Someone shouted for three cheers for Churchill. We raised our voices as much as we could, but it was a thin, ragged cheer from parched throats, dried by the acrid smoke billowing around us. Mr Churchill took off his hat and looked at us, his gaze coming to rest on our small group. We were only a few feet from him, and I saw the tears in his eyes.

Mr Harriman later reported that, when returning to London, Mr Churchill said: 'They have such confidence in me, I cannot let them down.'

On the Easter Sunday morning, the Dean, preaching in his damaged Cathedral, completed his sermon with the words 'after a Good Friday, there is always an Easter Sunday.'

Obviously, the military authorities knew that Bristol would be the target for that night, but did the Germans know that Mr Churchill was coming to the city, and did they think that he would be spending the night here? I have often wondered.

A child of the 1940s

R.M. Young

I held my Uncle's hand. 'You're trembling,' I said. 'No, I'm not,' he replied, 'I'm shivering, it's really cold.' I tried to look at his face, but he kept it turned away from me. It was after midnight, in June 1940, and we were standing in the garden of my home in Brislington, looking up at the night sky. It was not a warm night, but I thought, if a grown-up like Uncle was cold or trembling then there must be something to fear.

The siren had sounded half an hour before. That dismal, wailing sound had become so familiar in the last few months of air raid practices, but this was the first time there had been a real alert. When we heard the siren we hurried down the garden to the shelter. Father had worked hard to make it comfortable. He had made wooden bunks so that we could sleep there, all night if necessary. Mother had supplied the bed linen, a store of food, and a camping stove. It had been fun stocking up, but now it seemed different in the eerie darkness, with only a dim light from an oil lamp. However, the 'All Clear' had sounded almost at once, so we all came out and called to our neighbours, who laughed and joked that Jerry (the Germans) must have lost their way and it had all been a big mistake.

We returned to the house to make the obligatory pot of tea. That was when the noise started—the hum of aircraft engines, the scream of bombs falling, followed by explosions. We rushed into the garden, without thinking of the danger. Someone said later that Temple Meads Station had been the enemy's target.

That was the start of many days and nights spent listening to the sounds of aircraft overhead, of gun fire, of watching the pencil slim shafts of light from searchlights weaving patterns across the sky, of watching 'our' aeroplanes swoop across the skies and trying to get some sleep so that life could go on as usual.

Father joined the Fire Service and spent many nights on duty. Mother and I slept in the shelter every night. Sometimes a neighbour would join us with her young baby. The baby cried and cried and no-one got any sleep!

The days were as busy as the nights. Everyone helped those whose homes had been damaged, giving first aid, endless cups of tea, saving possessions and clearing rubble. There were shortages, queues, food was rationed, clothes needed coupons, Spam and whale meat arrived in the shops, some foods, such as bananas, were hardly seen at all. Children were sent to school, lessons and even examinations were sometimes taken in the shelters. Cookery lessons taught us to 'Eat More Potatoes' (a Government instruction), how to feed a family without meat and to cook with dried egg substitute! I walked to school through St George's Park, except when unexploded bombs were being detonated in the park, then a teacher would be at the park gates to send us home again. Home to an empty house, because all the mothers were at work, filling the jobs left vacant by the men in the Forces. My mother worked in the local jam factory, preparing fruit; in summer, strawberries and blackcurrants; in winter, marmalade.

Street party to celebrate the end of hostilities. Of the two teenage girls sitting at the table facing the camera, the author is the one on the left.

But there were many happy times. Father played the concertina on Sunday evenings in a concert party at the Ruskin Hall. He played the old songs and ballads that people loved to sing. The favourite was 'The Bells of St Mary's', which always reminded me of St Mary Redcliffe. Our neighbour sang 'So Deep is the Night, no moon tonight' and a wag shouted 'Good, Jerry won't be able to find us tonight.' I did a tap dance. The radio was our main source of entertainment and information. The news broadcasts were an important part of our day. We also listened to 'Lord Haw Haw' broadcasting in English from Germany. His broadcasts were propaganda designed to undermine our confidence. We laughed at him, especially when he predicted that Bristol's shopping area at Castle Street would be razed to the ground.

Soon, many streets had bomb damage and gaps in the rows of buildings. During one night raid the house opposite was bombed. All the windows in the houses on both sides of the street were shattered and glass was everywhere, inside and outside. No-one was hurt, the family were in their shelter. From the front the house did not appear to be badly damaged, but when you walked through the front door, there was nothing but a pile of rubble, only the front wall was standing. There was, however, part of the pantry shelf clinging to the wall and an egg in a bowl on the shelf. The egg was not even cracked.

Most nights when there was an air raid father was on duty, but he was at home on the night when an incendiary fell on our house. It was a bitterly cold night and the bomb came through the roof and caught the roof timbers alight. The fire watchers climbed through the trap door from the bathroom into the roof space with buckets and stirrup pump. The bath was kept permanently filled with water for just such an emergency. Mother and I stayed in the shelter, but I was worried about my budgerigar so Mother dashed into the house, picked up the cage and carried it to the shelter. The fire was soon put out and the bomb tossed into the street below through the hole in the roof. The fire watchers then moved on to another burning house and started all over again. Next morning we surveyed the damage. The bathroom floor was covered with ice, the roof timbers were badly burned and daylight could be seen through the roof. But the comradeship was always there, those more fortunate neighbours came along and helped to put a temporary cover over the gap until it was possible to get more permanent repairs. This could take some time as so many houses were being damaged.

This spirit of comradeship continued for many years. It was evident at the end of the War when everyone helped organise street parties on VE and VJ days. A photographic record of one such event appeared in the *Evening Post* at the time, and again recently. We have all gone our separate ways now, but I know I shall always remember the time when I was a child in Bristol in the 1940s.

The Reunion

B.F. Phillips

'There is a green hill far away . . .' so the old song goes and stirs the depth of many a memory with its lilting cadences and haunting words. For me the hill is neither green nor far away. In fact it is not even a hill, but in the mind's eye its shape thrusts itself through the mists of time as strongly and produces the same thrill of beloved memory as does the sacred hymn.

Nothing could be further from this mind's image of rural peace in reality. You see, the 'green hill' in my version is a red brick building which stands like a solemn sentinel guarding the entrance to St George's Park and which, on a mistless day, can be seen clear across the sprawling stretch of Bristol, from the heights of Ashley and Filton in the north to the roads escaping through Whitchurch to Wells in the south. To those contemporaries now living in its shadows it is identified as 'the Middle School of St George Comprehensive'—a modern description of convenience, a hook upon which to hang the fashionable phrase which concedes lip service to a system struggling to emulate its grand forbears. The term 'Middle School' applied to this great, ugly, many memoried, much loved building is a misnomer. There is nothing 'middle' about it. It has been, is and always will be to me 'St George Grammar School'. Grand in size and grander in achievement.

One March evening a few years ago, the doors of memory in eighty minds were thrust creakingly open to let the travellers in time wander thirty-one years down a road. At the road's end, in a few precious hours, we lived again those halcyon days peopled by our peers, mentors and guides which in that evening, if not present, were to be spirited forth in the telling of our tales. It was the night of the reunion.

For most of us that evening our last sight of those gathered there had been over thirty years ago when, on our way out through the gates of the school eager to step into a new world, we had shouted a hurried 'Cheerio and Good Luck'. Here we were again, older certainly, wiser maybe, but all full of the wonder of being present at the roll call again of the Class of '46 to '51.

I make no apologies for naming names. There is nothing bad or malicious which can ever be said of the Old Georgians or those custodians of their future who equipped them with the armour of knowledge for the uncharted journey through the world of growing up. As the passage of time was marked by our reminiscences in that evening the figures which peopled our memories beckoned us down the road of years. Doc Baldwin's short, gowned figure as he swept into the main hall to take morning service. The introductory bars of the day's chosen hymn played by a diminutive Miss Hayle, (fondly referred to as 'Daisy'—but always out of earshot!), from an elevation on the piano stool achieved by the use of the cushion which she regularly carried into Service. And there's Chas Waters, a stern figure with a Hitlerian moustache, harsh of voice and kind of nature whose position as Deputy Head ensured instant respect.

Morning Service has finished and with the intoned 'Amen' from five hundred voices to the daily prayer the clattering of as many pairs of varied shoes heralds the start of another day. The mists of time roll across memory's windows and for a moment those events which formed oases in the desert of scholastic routine begin to shimmer and recede. Was it Jack Randall who, from his entrenched position in the back row of two-beta, released a frog to hop down the aisle to the feet of Maude Mountney the French teacher? And is it true she picked it up and carried it backed to an amazed Randall? And I'm sure it was Derek Heal, the artist of the class, who enabled Sid Barnes, the teacher for the next period, to be confronted by the caricature of a fearsome prehistoric monster drawn on the blackboard and labelled 'Sidaurus Rex'. Did Sid ever rumble who it was?

Where has thirty-one years gone—and what difference does it make? The middling matrons of motherhood are fast disappearing, rounded paunches of respectable fatherhood, (and surfeit of beer), are dropping away succumbing to our recognition of each other, long forgotten phrases, the urgent beckoning of remembrances, all providing a heady brew of memories in that enchanted evening. The keepers of the records, our organising committee, who first invited us to enter forget-me-not lane, have done their work well. Copies of that most treasured of all relics, the school photograph, are given to each of us and with this as our magic carpet, our transport of delight, we again travel with each other as though it were yesterday.

Into the playground across the park to the fields of Whitehall. On the way a quick look into the church hall of St Ambrose where, every lunch hour—presiding over the male population of the school like disciples at the Last Supper—sat Doc Baldwin and staff. There, on the hall's stage seated at a cloth-draped trestle, those remote and lofty occupants of the staff common room revealed their earthly roots and shared the midday meal with their ravenous charges. With benevolent smile and air of ownership, like a contemporary but infinitely more kindly Bumble the Beagle, a green smocked Mrs Roach hovered behind the serving tables with her army of helpers preparing for the second great onslaught—the rush for 'seconds'—if any there were.

Let us proceed with our journey, stopping maybe for a penny 'vantas' at the small shop in Whitehall Road and having drunk our fill (or as much as our resources will allow), cross Gordon Road vying with each other for the loudest belch from that gaseous mixture, into that emerald green land of happily spent hours, Packer Playing Field. The seasons again parade before us. Autumn, Winter and Spring, the round and oval cases of soccer, rugby and hockey. Summer, the leather and willow of cricket, the bounce and twang of tennis. The sporting buffs holding various stages and audiences—Clive Henderson delivering his deadly fast ball to an imperturbable Mike Birbeck. The clown of the class, Brian Phillips, consigned to a distant position on the far boundary from where his raspberries and loony comments can cause minimal harm to the serious business of the last two periods of the day.

Glad memories, sad memories.

The annual sports day and a gloriously fleet footed runner carries off the honours. Charlie Barnett, athletic hero of the school and academician of the future—but never to become a 'leaver'. His death from poliomyelitis was to

The author at school.

be mourned by all before his last Speechgiving Day. But there were other, less tragic figures, for us newcomers to the school to revere. Len Green, hurling his javelin into space, seeming every inch the Greek God with his mane of golden hair. Johnny Stiff, beguiling the youthful acolytes of Rovers and City with his footwork.

And while these creatures of a higher order followed the lofty calling we newly arrived, lesser mortals, struggled to acquire the basic skills. Winter's first term and rugby training. Royston Abrahams, whose lusty farts caused much stifled mirth during morning service, became a *persona non grata* in the rugby scrum where the passage of any of his fabled spells of flatulence induced in his long suffering team mates an intense desire to win or concede the ball as soon as possible. Over this scene of striving and struggling, like a pillared White House guarding Presidential lawns, presides Whitehall Pavilion. Within its stuccoed walls on the upper floor is the Art Department, circled by boarded easels in front of paint splattered chairs, all to be swept to one side on the occasion of the school concert and annual speechgiving day. In his sawdust-covered kingdom on the ground floor, 'Pop' Lye administers the woodwork shop, endeavouring to impart the skills of carpenter and joiner to a student body whose resemblance to the material they are being taught to fashion is implied by more than one of the stalwart teaching staff in their daily strivings to create tomorrow's citizens.

Sadly, the hours of this magic evening have flown speedily as the past thirty or so years have been swept aside in these all too brief moments. The weight of the middle years settles again upon us and the farewells which we last wished each other from St George's Park gate on the threshold of our lives are echoed again in our goodnights. The evening of The Reunion may dim in our minds but in the years ahead the memories which it re-kindled will live on, as will our thoughts of the old school standing on the edge of St George's Park to which no greater honour could be paid than that accorded in the lines of the poem by John Betjeman:

'A gentle guest, a willing host,
Affection truly planted.
It's strange that those we miss the most
Are those we take for granted.'

39

My dad, the prostitute and the bank

Dorothy Whitehead

I used to wait for my friends by the Burke Statue on the centre most Tuesday nights, to go skating. It was the mid-sixties and as I used to wait there watching the traffic going round and round the centre I used to think that Bristol was the greatest place on earth. I told one of my elder cousins these thoughts but 'You won't damn well think so when you grow up!' came the reply.

Round about the same era we acquired a new neighbour opposite to us in our road in Eastville. Her name escapes me now but it doesn't really matter because our family had our own name for her—'Lady Madonna'—as in the Beatles' record of that time. You see the words of the song seemed to fit her exactly—she had a couple of kids, was Irish Catholic and, as we were soon to discover, was a prostitute. To my mum's great relief, she didn't practice her trade actually at the house. My sister and me loved it. It was by far the most exciting thing to have ever happened there. She would come out barefoot to sweep the steps and pavement. My mum would watch behind the net curtain and 'tut' in disgust. Curiously though, she possessed a strange kind of beauty with her long dark hair and bare feet, almost like a Cinderella from a Hippodrome pantomime waiting for her prince to come to take her away from the life she led.

But a more dramatic event was to come, more like something from a T.V. play than from a pantomime. Dad was upstairs one day having a snooze, not that he was lazy, you see, but bus driving schedules sometimes dictated a sleep during day-time hours. All of a sudden there were deep groans coming from his bedroom. Mum, my sister and me rushed upstairs and as we approached his bedroom door the words became clear, 'Get down, get her down!' When we burst into the bedroom dad was standing near the big bay window shouting at someone directly opposite and when we looked, there on the upstairs window ledge was 'Madonna'—barefoot and staring at the ground below. Perhaps she had grown tired of waiting for her Prince Charming. Mary, my sister, ran across the road to the house, despite orders from mum, 'You're not going in there!'

Mary was good with people and in no time at all had talked her down and they were both sat at the kitchen table talking about things in general. After that little episode things unfortunately slipped back to normal again.

Just like children of sailors listening to their father's seafaring tales, when we were kids we used to listen to tales from our dad's bus routes; about the little old ladies who would call him 'sonny' and other characters who frequented his bus. One macabre tale was about a 'bad' bus that seemed to bring death or injury to all who crossed its path, be it drivers, pedestrians, passengers or mechanics, until it came to the point when the bus company just had to take it off the road and quarantine it at the depot. Looking back now, I don't think for one moment that there was any truth in these shivery little tales and, come to think of it, whenever dad used to take me up to Eastville Depot 'The Big Bad Bus' was always conveniently 'missing' that

Above: Fairfax House during demolition:
'A memory with each dusty load'.
(Photograph: B.U.P.)
Below: The author with older sister Mary.

day. But we loved the story and made dad tell it again and again. Mind you, whenever I go to a transport museum or bus rally I always cast a very cautious eye over any old green buses, circa 1956.

As well as spinning yarns my dad also had a gift for imitating gossiping middle-aged women, in a sort of Les-Dawson-type way, but with a Bristolian accent. This, too, was picked up from observing bus passengers. But my favourite bit of naughtiness from dad was, when on returning from our annual day-trip to Weston, he would walk up the road fantasizing about the 'plane journey' and how rough the 'take-off' had been, and how nice it was of the 'pilot' to invite him into the cock-pit. Then about the waiter in the fictitious hotel and commenting on the extortionate prices of the cocktails. All this would be said within earshot of any gossips who might be in their front gardens, in the hope that they would think we had been somewhere really plush, not just Weston-super-Mare, and in the hope that these false snippets of information would add fuel to their next round of chit-chat. We used to walk behind him giggling and trying to hide.

Then, after a poor but happy childhood, I got my first job, with Lloyds Bank, Eastville, and at the age of 20, upon my marriage, was transferred to Merchant Street Branch, in the heart of Broadmead. The bank was housed at numbers 19-21, a quaint little listed building which in the past had been an alms-house. Some remedial work had to be carried out while I was there, on a leaky window frame, which had become rather distressed-looking with age and possessed a rather uneven slope. The contract builder was told that because it was a listed building the new window frame must look exactly like the old one and the builder's reply came, 'Blimey, weve got some bad chippies but not as bad as that!' I worked there for seven years—some of the happiest days of my life. I have always liked Broadmead. As a young girl that was the place to go with my mum or sister on a Saturday afternoon. It was the place where we would do our Christmas shopping.

On Tuesday, May 10th, last year, I stood on Union Street Bridge with my husband and nine year old son and watched the men scoop away the rubble that used to be Fairfax House and part of Woolworth's. My little boy found the experience quite exciting but for me there was a big lump in my throat as I felt that, along with the rubble, parts of me were being hauled up onto the tip-up trucks. I could recall a memory with each dusty load. There was one consolation though, at least 'my' bank won't meet with the same fate, not for a long time anyway, as it is to be incorporated into the new shopping mall, so at least that part of me will live on for a while.

On May 19th, I watched the demolition of the Canons Marsh warehouses. Another Lloyds Bank is going to be built there and perhaps the new building will supply me with future memories if I ever decide to resume my banking career. And do you know, after all these years, and at the grand old age of 36, and having travelled near and far, I still think that Bristol is the greatest place on earth, and so do certain financial institutions, so it seems, but then maybe it's because I'm a Bristolian . . .

If you can't take a joke . . .

Colin Dean

The City of Bristol had its own police force until 1974 when it was swallowed up in the present Avon and Somerset force. Its helmet badge carried the City crest but it had its own unofficial motto. Just when everything seemed to be going against you, the voice of a colleague would pipe up, 'if you can't take a joke you shouldn't have joined'.

In 1955 I joined a force without panda cars or radios, when the traffic department at St John's Bridge (near today's Froomsgate House) had Wolseleys, inspectors could drive Morris Minors, selected divisional PCs could ride BSA 250s or Triumph 500 motorcycles, but patrolling officers had black lace-up boots and black sit-up-and-beg bicycles. Communication was by police pillars, blue telephone boxes with a light atop which flashed when a bobby was needed, and a direct line to the station for any member of the public strong enough to be able to open the springloaded door.

Police work was then, as now, mainly about trouble, people in it or people who had got it. You just couldn't let it get to you. One bitterly cold winter's night, on foot patrol from Fishponds Station, I tried to shelter from the wind behind a telephone kiosk in Manor Road. We had a choice of protective clothing, including a very heavy, almost ankle length, greatcoat and a cape. On this night I was wearing both, over a uniform jacket that buttoned up to the neck, sweater, scarf and pyjama trousers under the thick serge issue. I heard voices approaching but was very shocked when they suddenly smashed some glass in the kiosk I was leaning on. They were surprised to see me, too, but recovered quickly and began to leg it. Well, I did my best, but with all that clothing . . . I had lost them and in final desperation shouted 'Stop or I fire'. And they did. They were just realising that foot patrol officers in Fishponds were unlikely to be armed when I caught them.

There were quite a lot of people who actually wanted to be arrested, particularly at night. They tended to be lonely and seemed to relish the attention, and perhaps the warmth of police stations. One night, as I climbed Christmas Steps, a figure suddenly leapt out of a shop doorway and said, 'OK, you got I, caught I redhanded, fair enough'. I asked him what I had caught him doing. 'Breaking into this shop'. The shop was secure. 'You haven't', I said. 'I have' he insisted, and so we argued. I refused to arrest him and told him to go away. Later on, the pillar in Park Row near St Michael's Hill was flashing. It was the station sergeant at Nelson Street, to say 'Your prisoner is in the station, where the hell are you?'

The *Western Daily Press* featured in a similar story. A young lady went to the central police station in Nelson Street and complained that her husband had assaulted her. She was not pleased to be told that it was a civil matter, not something for the police, so went next door to the *Post* and *Press* offices, on the corner of Silver Street and Broadmead. Now at one o'clock in the morning, the presses were really humming, printing that morning's edition and the night editor rang the station asking could she be removed. It didn't sound too serious but the editor told me that she was delaying the printing

Author Colin Dean aged nineteen in night duty uniform of choker collar and black helmet badge 'so as not to show up too brightly and disturb criminals!'

and causing a nuisance. Apparently no one took any notice of her allegations until she began showing them the 'evidence', which was on a part of her anatomy which seemed suddenly to arouse interest in the night staff, all of them. Had the *WDP* been contemplaing a page three feature, she would have been an excellent candidate but the editor was worried about late deliveries.

Such incidents were tasks for policewomen so I took her to that department and they began making enquiries about her, while she kept telling me she was going to 'have me' in a minute. I was getting worried, I was young and it was nearly breakfast time! In the end it was discovered that she had done this before and it had ended with her causing serious injury to any man who reacted to her advances.

It poured with rain one night in July 1968 but it was fine and sunny when I left home for an 8 a.m. start at Bedminster Station in East Street. It wasn't until I reached Bedminster Parade that I came across a bit of flooding. When I entered the yard at the back of the station, opposite Wills Hall, there were several rowing boats moored. I waded into the station where the inspector told me to take two men and row in one of those boats to Duckmoor Road, Ashton and see what could be done to help. I thought he was joking but he was an inspector so he couldn't have been! Now I could have walked or driven there but what route do you take by boat? Our seamanship wasn't so good so we waded along Coronation Road pulling the boat until we reached Ashton Gate where the flooding was deeper.

Each boat crew had a street to ensure that we could account for everyone. Most people were confined to their upstairs rooms and we contributed more to the raising of morale with our antics in the water than to any heroics. One old lady was found still sitting in her favourite armchair, with water at chest level. We wanted to take her to safety but she told us she had lived through worse than this in two world wars. Her only requirement was that her television had stopped working and if we could fix it she would be fine. We took her for a ride in our boat. Now that *did* worry her.

In a city like Bristol, water is never far away so all police officers had to be able to swim and lifesave. Those who couldn't had to attend at Jacob Wells Baths at 8 a.m. in the mornings until they could. But they didn't teach you about the River Avon mud. One day a woman was spotted stuck in the mud. With a couple of colleagues I attended and found her quite a way from the bank and up to her waist in mud, and shouting for help. We started to wade out to her but we too began to sink. I mentioned that I had seen somewhere that we should crawl along the mud to avoid sinking and the others volunteered me to try it. Well I didn't sink but it was hard work, smelly, uncomfortable and progress was slow. It wasn't helped by my colleagues becoming impatient, wading past me and pulling her out!

What were you doing, we asked her. Trying to end it all, she replied. Then why did you call for help, we asked. I wanted to drown, not sink in mud and when I started walking to the water's edge I didn't realise the tide was going out, too quick for me to catch it, she replied. That wasn't the end of it for me. They wouldn't allow me back in the patrol car in my filthy state. They marched me to the nearest house, along the Portway, and hosed me down. And what did they say as they were doing it? If you can't take a joke . . .

Tapping up in the Sixties

Rosalind Anstey

Once upon a time there were two teenaged girls, me and my mate Val, who suddenly realised that there was life beyond the confines of Pill and Portishead when I moved to Brislington and saw the pubs with all those BOYS. So, to the accompaniment of Rock 'n Roll, The Beatles and Trad Jazz we decided to explore the night life of Bristol.

Luckily, my mate Val was good at tapping up blokes. I just tagged along, being the shy and retiring sort. Thinking back, we must have been a sight for sore eyes as we tottered around on our six-inch stilettos with our African Violet swagger coats slung back off the shoulders. Val had her hair in regulation Cilla Black style while I tried to no avail to straighten my unruly mop into the same style. I had to settle for a black ribbon and, when I passed a building site and the lads yelled out 'Hey Dusty' (Dusty Springfield to the uninitiated), it made my day. (Cilla Black clones, eat your heart out).

Dances were a good place to meet BOYS with one being on nearly every night of the week. The Glen was like another world. All the girls would prepare their hair in front of pink, gilded lacquer-spotted mirrors and chatter excitedly about the local talent they had spied coming in. A big sparkling globe spun round on the ceiling casting images . . . images of girls bopping away with their frilly, silly blouses, Chanel-style suits and flat ballerina shoes . . . images of Dave Prowse leaning against the wall with his giant figure stuffed into a dark suit, horn-rimmed glasses making him look like Buddy Holly, and huge, thick shoes. Rumour had it that if you jumped on his feet he would be in so much pain that you could do anything you liked with him. We didn't try it. A puny little Eric Morley was manager before going on to greater things. Chinese Jazz, at the Coin Exchange, was different again. Uncle Bonny would bounce around in his straw boater with joss sticks in his hands.

We thought we were cool as we danced in our brightly coloured shifts and black polo jumpers and black stockings. Many good bands appeared there, from Alexis Korner with what must have been Charlie Watts on drums (pre Stones days) to Terry Lightfoot, who chatted me up at half time in the Rummer asking me to come back to his hotel room for coffee. I was sorely tempted. He was FAMOUS. But modesty prevailed (I was a coward). I said no.

Another haunt, the Grand Spa at Clifton, was boring, with a boring band, boring girl singer and boring 'bright young things'. But I actually struck lucky one night when this blonde student approached me. 'Here Val. He's got a car. What shall I do?' 'Go on, Ros. He looks safe enough.' So, I did, and I didn't. His smashing little MG beckoned, then I noticed the lack of windscreen. A slight prang, this student-type said. Thinking of my carefully lacquered hair and the sight it would look after a battle with the breeze, I gracefully declined (chickened out again). Other dances consisted of the Blue Notes at The Ship, Avon Cities at the Riccoco, a little dug-out tunnelling off Leonards Lane, and of course our Acker at the Crown.

The author second from right with teenage friends.

Then we had pubs with the Greyhound at Broadmead leading the way. Saturday lunchtimes we would pile in after working 'till midday and stand posing by the doorway of one of the many side bars, a mug of lukewarm bitter in our hand. Then off we would go to the Byron Coffee bar to sober up until one day we made the mistake of taking little Scouse Johnny. He put whiskey in his coffee. An irate little Greek bore down on us, waving his arms in the air and gesticulating. We presumed he wanted us out. He did. Silly little scouse git. 'Wasn't my fault' he said. The Inkerman we liked with its pictures of different uniformed soldiers hung on the walls and of course its jukebox. The Landlord was a very smart upright ex-Grenadier guard who didn't stand any nonsense but he always had a full pub. The Bear and Ragged Staff, on the other hand, we heard was rough. We didn't believe the rumours. It was a beautiful, old 17th century pub and had a long bar with tiled walls. The jukebox played 'Love, love me do' by the Beatles. We were in heaven . . . until a teddyboy went flying past at fifty miles an hour on the end of someone else's fist.

The Rummer had lots of dimly lit little bars underground with glass balls hanging in nets from the walls. We would get Chanel No 5 at sixpence a squirt in the Ladies and then go on the hunt. Patrick Troughton, minus his Doctor Who scarf, spent one evening there with some dubious looking friends and Charles Grey even asked us the time with his perfectly modulated voice. Then some balloonists asked us if we wanted to join them on a balloon ride *under* the Suspension Bridge, we declined. This was pre-Ashton Court days, after all. Some producer types even asked us if we would like to go ski-ing. We said yes, never thinking they would turn up. I mean . . . where would one ski in Bristol. *They turned up*, bearing skis on top of their tiny Mini. We weren't home when they rang. The Cellar Bar was also popular if you didn't mind being squeezed to death (a good way of meeting the opposite sex) or the odd fight being thrown in sometimes. After the last fight we saw there it was highly entertaining to see eight teddyboys squeeze into a bubble car, *shut the door*, and drive with no sign of a snorkel to breath with or a telescope to guide them. We even tried the Shakespeare at Prince Street, and were refused a drink. 'We do not serve young ladies with scrumpy' the stout landlady said. If we were lucky and a fella asked us out for a meal, it would definitely have to be the Rummer, Llandoger or Steak and Stilton. These were romantic, cosy, intimate places with candles discreetly placed on tables. This was alright if you fancied the bloke but otherwise we would go to the Tavern in Clifton and watch the world go by through the little tunnelled entrance.

But, after all the places we tried, it was at a cinema that I met my future 'love'. The Ritz changed my life as a handsome teddyboy bought my love with a Choc-ice as he joined me one night.

So it is that all good things come to an end.

Wartime spirit, without war

Glenn Vowles

Bristol is a city steeped in history. There are many developments which are rapidly changing its face, like its fast growing influence as a financial centre, that also bring frustratingly difficult problems. So while historic achievements, people and events should not be dismissed, history should not bind us. There is much to be found that could bind us. To adapt to accelerating change we should all look forward, but learn from the past.

During wartime and deprivation great comradeship existed. Now apathy, cynicism, and materialism are surely destroying more than all the bombs that have fallen on Bristol. Indeed we may be bound by history. Divisions between black and white, rich and poor, are evident. People are physically separated by a road system which ignores community life.

The community spirit and friendliness found in the St Philips Marsh area up to its break-up in the late 1950s gives us much to emulate. The closeness is needed, without the poverty, clannish suspicion of outsiders and the sexism of the times. Perhaps we need wartime spirit without war.

Elements found in the old St Philips Marsh—the shops in every street, the local small businesses and self-employed chimney sweeps, blacksmiths, wet fish sellers—should be recreated. The principle of self-contained, but not isolated communities, with local people providing themselves with goods and services, is good.

Working and living environments have changed. We now have fairly clean, though not perfect, drinking water whereas in the 12th century when Bristol was a major wine port the poor quality of the water was cited as a reason for drinking wine! In St Philips developing industry brought jobs, housing and so people. Industry also brought its foul smells, river pollution and noise. Indeed, eventually the people were squeezed out, used then disposed, by growing industry.

The community there was crushed. Future Bristol must have industry to meet people's needs not people that service industry, only to be moved 'out of town'.

Housing in Bristol has moved from the contrast of huge, plush Victorian places with small, cramped and basic utility housing, to council estates and flats sadly lacking in wildlife and open space. The plush housing is still there, the housing problems are different, if not worse, people now at the mercy of 'mysterious' market forces. Lack of self determination in local areas, or even a lack of any say at all, needs putting right. This would avoid the breakdown of communities and shed light on the needs and problems of areas, like housing and open space needs.

To this day Bristol's notorious but profitable role in the slave trade (white slavery since the time of the Norman conquest, then later black slavery up to the 1800s) influences the view many have of the present, even the future. People said that slavery was intimately entwined with the economy of Bristol. Indeed, much money was involved but slavery was abolished. Bristol's present South African trade links via the port are profitable too.

Will this last as slavery did?

Bristol's economy has been served by people. Sherry, tobacco and chocolate firms run by God-fearing families employed thousands and still do. The wealth divisions evident from history still exist today. Compare house prices North and South of the river. Wealthy merchants had the legal advice and protection of Latchams, Montague and Niblett, Britain's longest surviving law firm. They bought jewels from Bristol Bridge and sent for fresh meat from Temple Gate. Brooks dyed ostrich feathers for Bristol ladies. Exploitation today has some historic roots, even if different situations are involved.

Bristol's future economy should be built on the theme of reconciliation. Small firms, with work self-contained and flexible, would reconcile material needs with creative needs if local people produced for their own needs. A strong element of worker and community control with local reinvestment and recirculation of resources is the more just and equal Bristol I want. Elements of this future can be found in the past but never all the required features.

Reconciliation of the need for economic activity and a clean and pleasant environment to live in is a must. Pollution from industry in St Philips Marsh in the past and at Avonmouth today shows that ecological concerns have still to be considered of primary importance.

Cars in today's Bristol bring pollution, stress and disfigurement to historic buildings like St Mary Redcliffe Church. Who today wants this magnificent building encircled by crowded, hostile roads? Do we want to go on hearing of 'lots of traffic chaos due to temporary lights at Whitchurch Lane. Wells Road and Bath Road very busy and flowing slowly' on local radio every day?

It is not only for reasons of nostalgia that I like the idea of trams, or something like them, returning to Bristol. The Metro idea is a good one. If properly planned with local people it will provide a great service. It should be integrated with a bus and rail system. Park-and-ride schemes, more cycleways and more pedestrian-only should prosper too. The car rules too many lives, when we should rule the car.

Future Bristol will I hope reconcile people with each other and their surroundings. Its people will be aware of Bristol as a whole from within their own diverse self-reliant communities. Bristol's inter-dependence within Britain and the World should be recognised. People will, I hope, be happier and use leisure wisely. Others, too, will enjoy the quality of Bristol, historic city.

Extras

Phil Smith

There I was in Bristol Cathedral. And the pillars were crashing down everywhere around us. Smashes and crashes and a nerve splitting splintering sound of accident and tragedy approaching like apocalyptic horses in harness. I turned and ran towards the sound, rushing back into camera shot to tear at the wreckage. The screaming floor manager froze. I looked up. The 'dead and injured' beneath the masonry were neither dead nor injured. In fact the masonry was not masonry, but what I was tearing at was coming away in my hands rather too easily—balsa wood and stretched canvas. I looked, like the fool I was playing, straight into the camera lens and formed a big, stupid 'O' with my lips.

I hid. I don't know whether it was me or not, but someone ruined that 'take' on the set of *The Medusa Touch*—stars; Richard Burton and Lee Remick— director; Jack Gold. I was an extra. I'd done as I'd been told along with the other five hundred of us packed into the nave of Bristol Cathedral. I'd panicked to order. But when the balsa wood pillar had fallen it had caught my eye and then my imagination. That Hollywood magic had cast its spell over me and I'd gone to the assistance of stuntmen who needed my help like the first jockey past the post needs a Steward's Enquiry. 'Cut! Cut!' I could hear a furious voice shouting. I was hiding behind a real stone pillar by then. They had to come back weeks later and do the shot again.

It was the strangest job I've ever done. My mate had to ring a Lady Somebody, who was very annoyed we had her number, but gave us an address in Clifton and a time, where and when we found a queue the length of the street, at the end of which there was a man who said we didn't have the letter we needed.

'But Lady .... sent us!'

'Oh very well, but that's the last ones without letters.'

Fifteen pounds a night. From 10pm till 4am. I fell asleep at work on the third day after the night before. But we were stars—we could have all the hamburgers we could eat (we thought). But the trouble with cinema is that it's 1% filming and 99% boredom. We played every time-passing game there is.

'I'm so thrilled,' said a woman from Hartcliffe with a purple rinse. Cold, full of coffee and three hours since the last 'take', we called her 'Mrs Thrill'. We were thrilled too, really—we larked about, leapt in front of the camera on every crowd shot, thanks to youth and good timing, managed to appear four times standing on the same wall in the same tracking shot.

My clearest memory, though, of those chilly, but warm inside, times with Mrs Thrill and co. is of the last night. This was at a time when the old Royal Hotel at the bottom of Park Street was still open and we were fed, before shooting started, in a canteen at the back of the Hotel. Now, being extras, some of us (mentioning no names) had been queueing up for more than one meal. A system of chitties had been introduced. No chitty, no meal.

That night they were filming the arrival of the Royal Person, about whose ears the evil kinetic wizard of the film, Richard Burton, was to bring the stones of the Cathedral. When we collected our chitty many of us were given uniforms, robes or ermine. I wasn't. I went for a drink in The Way Inn. When I came out I saw a sight which has remained with me ever since. For there, in the road at the back of the Royal, queued up at a mobile canteen, plates and chitties in hand, were generals, chief constables, bishops, admirals, lords and ladies, judges and royals. There it was—the whole British Establishment! Queueing up for its gruel! With plate and chitty in hand!

Now, when times are grim and it's hard to feel the irresponsible optimism of Mrs Thrill, when vicious laws and taxes and sackings are imposed with no pillars being brought down—stone or canvas—I remember what I saw behind the Royal. And I think to myself—one day, one day.

Something about the authors

FRED CATLEY

Fred Catley worked at George's, the Park Street booksellers, from 1928. In 1956 he was made a director, and in 1976 he retired. Through World War II he lived in a top-floor flat in Clifton, and moved to Woollard for 1945-1957. He has lived in Whitchurch village ever since.

DANNY PRICE

Danny Price was born in St Philips. He was a Bristol Councillor from 1936 until he joined the army in 1939, and served as a chindit with Wingate in Burma. He discovered he could write at the age of seventy four, and since then he has written twelve short stories and poems.

CYNTHIA FLOYD

Cynthia Floyd, a retired Civil Servant, often uses reminiscences of her ninety two year old mother, Gladys, with whom she lives, in her hobby of writing.

HENRY BELCHER

Henry Belcher was brought up in Salisbury Road and attended Downend Church of England School. He now lives in Westerleigh.

ALBERT McGRATH

Albert McGrath was born the son of a miner in South Wales in 1920. He was brought up by his grandmother in Bristol, and lived in Lebec House in Dowry Parade, Hotwells, until he was twenty. In 1941 he was conscripted by the army and joined the Royal Armoured Corps, serving in the Middle East. He was a docker at Avonmouth Docks from 1953 to 1968 and now is the Chairman of Avonmouth Community Council.

ANGELA TIPPETTS

Angela Tippetts was born and bred in Bristol. She was educated at Fairfield Grammar School. Now a widow, she has two grown-up children. She enjoys writing articles, stories and plays for W.I. Currently, she is the secretary of Yatton Moor P.C.C.

JOAN COOMBS

Joan Coombs has lived in Bristol all her life, mostly in the Speedwell area. She likes vegetable gardening, writing, talking and reading.

GLORIA REED

Gloria Reed is married with two grown-up children. She is a teacher in a Bristol Infants' School and lives in Coalpit Heath.

JOYCE WILLIAMS

Joyce Williams was born in Bristol and educated at Redland High School. She is now a widow with a stepson. During the war she served in a street First Aid Party, and subsequently in Warden's Service. Her hobbies are reading, writing short stories, listening to classical music, gardening and finding out about local history.

R.M. YOUNG
Renee Young was born in 1928, and educated at St George Grammar School. She is married with a son and a daughter, and is a retired lecturer of secretarial subjects. Her interests include Bridge, antiques and pottery.

B.F. PHILIPS
Brian Philips was born in 1934 in St Andrews, Bristol. He was educated at Sefton Park School and St George Grammar School. Apart from his time in National Service and two years spent in Uganda, Brian Philips has lived in Bristol and worked for British Telecom.

DOROTHY WHITEHEAD
Dorothy Whitehead was born in Bristol in 1952, to Harold and Annie Stokes. She was a bank clerk for eleven years, and now lives in Warmley with her husband and son.

COLIN DEAN
Colin Dean was born in Poole and moved to Bristol when he joined the Police force from school in 1955. Despite experiences such as he describes, he managed to survive until 1970. He has been Avon County Council's road safety officer since 1974, and now lives in Olveston.

ROSALIND ANSTEY
Rosalind Anstey lives in Pensford and is married with two teenage children. Her hobbies include local history, photography, family history, writing and music.

GLENN VOWLES
Glenn Vowles, from Knowle, is twenty-seven, and married to Ann. He attended Merrywood School and is self-employed. He was a Green General Election Candidate in 1987.

PHIL SMITH
Phil Smith lives in Bedminster and is a member of Bedminster Area Housing Committee of Council Tenants and the Secretary of Windmill Hill Labour Party. He has also worked as a writer, co-ordinator of Bristol Broadsides (Co-op) and as a porter at Bristol Central Library. He now works as a warehouseman.

Something about Redcliffe

Redcliffe have now published more than 50 books about Bristol. In this we are almost certainly unique both in having produced so many books about a single town, and in dealing with such a wide diversity of aspects.

Indeed, with the possible exception of London, no British town has been as well documented as Bristol.

In our list, you will find several books of personal reminiscence. These are more than exercises in nostalgia. They are tomorrow's history in the making. We have published books, too, on Bristol's rich architectural and artistic heritage, on its famous associations, on the historic harbour and on local industries. With many of these we, and our authors, have worked closely with the City's Museum & Art Gallery or with sponsors, as some of these books could not have been published at popular prices without the enlightened support of local businesses.

In all, Redcliffe have published over one hundred books, from poetry to sport, as well as a strong West Country list. If you would like a copy of our catalogue, please ask.

The following are just a few of our many books about the city.

BRISTOL & CO
Helen Reid £4.95
The city's commercial history over the past 200 years traced through biographies of old established Bristol firms—from butchers to stockbrokers.

BRISTOL BEYOND THE BRIDGE
Michael Manson £4.95
The turbulent story of Redcliffe, Temple and St Thomas from the Middle Ages to today.

IMAGES OF BRISTOL
Victorian photographers at work.
James Belsey & David Harrison £4.95
Outstanding Victorian and Edwardian photographs provide a living portrait of Bristol in the nineteenth century, and show the Victorian's fascination with the romantic image, street life, invention and industry.

BRISTOL OBSERVED
J.H. Bettey £4.95
Innumerable visitors to Bristol have, over the centuries, noted their reactions to the city. *Bristol Observed* offers penetrating insights from famous observers like Cromwell and J.B. Priestly to the lesser known, such as Elizabethan soldiers and itinerant preachers.

BRISTOL: THE GROWING CITY
Edited by David Harrison £4.95
An affectionate look at how Bristol has grown and changed, written by a group of leading local journalists.

HUNGRY FIGHTERS OF THE WEST
Edited by David Foot £4.95
Evocative look at the lives of famous West Country fighters in and around the boxing ring in the 1920s and '30s. Told in their own words and setting the sport in a context of social deprivation.

THE FORGOTTEN FRONT: BRISTOL AT WAR 1914-1918
James Belsey £1.95
Bristol at war was a transformed city. This book presents a true picture of the full tragic impact of the Great War on the city.

BRISTOL BETWEEN THE WARS
Edited by David Harrison £4.95
Bristol seen through the eyes of those who lived through two decades of change, richly illustrated with contemporary photographs.

A CITY AND ITS CINEMAS
Charles Anderson £2.95
The fantastic story of the rise and fall of Bristol's picture houses.

BRISTOL BLITZ DIARY
John Dike £2.95
A chilling insight into the air raids on the city from an old diary discovered by chance.

BRISTOL BLITZ: THE UNTOLD STORY
Helen Reid £3.95
A picture of Bristol and its people at war, with many photographs never before printed because of wartime censorship.

BRISTOL IN THE FIFTIES
Edited by James Belsey £4.95
A team of Bristol's best writers recall life in Bristol as it was 30 to 40 years ago.